BRUCE LEE

A Real-Life Reader Biography

Wayne Wilson

Mitchell Lane Publishers, Inc.
P.O. Box 619
Bear, Delaware 19701

Second Printing

Real-Life Reader Biographies

Paula Abdul	Christina Aguilera	Marc Anthony	Lance Armstrong
Drew Barrymore	Jan & Stan Berenstain	Tony Blair	Brandy
Garth Brooks	Kobe Bryant	Sandra Bullock	Mariah Carey
Aaron Carter	Cesar Chavez	Roberto Clemente	Christopher Paul Curtis
Roald Dahl	Oscar De La Hoya	Trent Dimas	Celine Dion
Sheila E.	Gloria Estefan	Mary Joe Fernandez	Michael J. Fox
Andres Galarraga	Sarah Michelle Gellar	Jeff Gordon	Mia Hamm
Melissa Joan Hart	Salma Hayek	Jennifer Love Hewitt	Faith Hill
Hollywood Hogan	Katie Holmes	Enrique Iglesias	Allen Iverson
Janet Jackson	Derek Jeter	Steve Jobs	Michelle Kwan
Bruce Lee	Jennifer Lopez	Cheech Marin	Ricky Martin
Mark McGwire	Alyssa Milano	Mandy Moore	Chuck Norris
Tommy Nuñez	Rosie O'Donnell	Mary-Kate and Ashley Olsen	Rafael Palmeiro
Gary Paulsen	Colin Powell	Freddie Prinze, Jr.	Condoleezza Rice
Julia Roberts	Robert Rodriguez	J.K. Rowling	Keri Russell
Winona Ryder	Cristina Saralegui	Charles Schulz	Arnold Schwarzenegger
Selena	Maurice Sendak	Dr. Seuss	Shakira
Alicia Silverstone	Jessica Simpson	Sinbad	Jimmy Smits
Sammy Sosa	Britney Spears	Julia Stiles	Ben Stiller
Sheryl Swoopes	Shania Twain	Liv Tyler	Robin Williams
Vanessa Williams	Venus Williams	Tiger Woods	

Library of Congress Cataloging-in-Publication Data
Wilson, Wayne, 1953-
    Bruce Lee/Wayne Wilson.
       p. cm.—(A real-life reader biography)
    Includes index.
    ISBN 1-58415-066-1
    1. Lee, Bruce, 1940-1973—Juvenile literature. 2. Actors—United States—Biography—Juvenile literature. 3. Martial artists—United States—Biography—Juvenile literature. [1. Lee, Bruce, 1940-1973. 2. Actors and actresses. 3. Martial artists.] I. Title. II. Series.
PN2287.L2897 W55 2001
791.43′028′092—dc21
   [B]
                                         00-067802

ABOUT THE AUTHOR: Wayne Wilson was born and raised in Los Angeles. He received a Master of Arts in Education from the University of California, Los Angeles with a specialization in Sociology and Anthropology. For 16 years he was co-owner and president of a pioneering and innovative publishing company specializing in multicultural designs. Wilson completed interviews with influential Latino men throughout the country and wrote over 160 biographies for *Encuentros: Hombre A Hombre*, a comprehensive vocational education book that was published by the California Department of Education in 2001.

PHOTO CREDITS: cover: Shooting Star; p. 4 Shooting Star; pp. 6, 14 Corbis; p. 17 Globe Photos; p. 18 Shooting Star; p. 20 AP; p. 21 Kobal; p. 22 Globe Photos.

ACKNOWLEDGMENTS: The following story has been thoroughly researched, and to the best of our knowledge, represents a true story. While every possible effort has been made to ensure accuracy, the publisher will not assume liability for damages caused by inaccuracies in the data, and makes no warranty on the accuracy of the information contained herein.

Table of Contents

Chapter 1
The Greatest Martial Arts Star

Bruce Lee's dream was that one day he would be an international superstar. In early 1969, when he was 28 years old, he wrote the master plan for his life on a piece of paper. In it he made a prediction: "I, Bruce Lee, will be the highest paid Oriental superstar in the United States. In return, I will give the most exciting performances and render the best of quality in the capacity of an actor."

Not long after this declaration, Bruce began to achieve the success that he had predicted. But unfortunately, he never saw the full impact of his

Bruce Lee's dream was to be an international superstar.

accomplishments. On July 20, 1973, he tragically died at the young age of 32, only one month before the premiere of his famous film, *Enter the Dragon*, at Hollywood's famous Grauman's Chinese Theater. The movie made him an international superstar and is regarded as a classic of action movies.

Bruce Lee revolutionized the martial arts industry and did more to bring the fighting arts to the general public than any other person in the 20th century. Martial arts schools throughout

Bruce was known for his superfast flying kicks. This is a scene from the movie Fists of Fury, *1971.*

the world were filled with eager students who were inspired by Lee's fighting style. The martial arts movie industry exploded with many films that tried to duplicate Bruce's success.

In real life, Bruce was nearsighted, only stood 5'7" and weighed about 140 pounds. But on the movie screen, he looked much larger with tight, well-defined muscles, like a giant poised to spring into action. His warrior cry was usually followed by high-flying kicks and fast punches. Fans returned to the theaters to see him perform.

Today, largely due to Lee's influence, the martial arts are regularly used in both television and movies. Bruce Lee opened the doors for action stars like Chuck Norris, Steven Seagal, and Jackie Chan.

Bruce Lee is the yardstick by which everyone else is measured. His status is legendary and his image is displayed around the world. Millions of people who have never seen any of his five movies know his name.

In real life, Bruce was 5' 7" tall and weighed about 140 pounds.

Chapter 2
The Little Dragon

From the moment of his birth it seemed Bruce Lee was destined for greatness. He was born in San Francisco's Chinatown on November 27, 1940, right at the start of the Year of the Dragon. In her book *The Bruce Lee Story* (published in 1989), his wife Linda Lee describes Bruce as being "a remarkable and unique child, with tremendous burning energy." His Chinese nickname "Mo Si Tung" translates in English as "Never Sits Still."

At the time of his birth, Bruce's father, Lee Hoi Chuen, a popular Chinese film and stage actor, was

Bruce Lee's father was a popular Chinese film and stage actor.

performing comedy on stage in New York's Chinatown with the touring Cantonese Opera Company of Hong Kong. His mother, Grace, who was of Chinese and German descent, named him Lee Jun Fan, which means "return again" because she believed Bruce would one day return to his birthplace, San Francisco. A hospital nurse suggested his English name, Bruce.

After the tour ended, the Lees went back to their two-bedroom apartment in Hong Kong. The full household consisted of Bruce's parents, his sisters Phoebe and Agnes, his brothers Peter and Robert, servants, and an assortment of animals. The Lees had been a show-business family for many years and it was through his father's connections that Bruce became a child film star.

His screen career began at the age of six in a movie made in Hong Kong called *The Beginning of a Boy*. Two years later he acted in his second film, where he was known as Lee Siu Lung (The

Bruce's film career began when he was six years old.

Little Dragon), the name by which he became best known throughout Asia.

By the time he was 18, Lee had appeared in 20 films and was a teen idol in Hong Kong. His last role as a child actor was a 1958 film called *The Orphan*. It was about street gangs in Hong Kong and Bruce could draw on his own experience.

The streets of Hong Kong were a rough place to grow up. Gangs of Chinese youth roamed the streets and Bruce ran with them. He admitted to *Black Belt Magazine* in October 1967 that, "As a kid in Hong Kong, I was a punk and went looking for fights. Then one day I wondered what would happen if I didn't have my gang behind me if I got into a fight. I decided to learn how to protect myself."

So Bruce's parents enrolled him in kung fu (Chinese boxing) classes. He was 13 years old when he studied with renowned Sifu (instructor) Yip Man.

Lee not only excelled in kung fu, he became obsessed with it. It wasn't

By the time Bruce was 18 years old, he had appeared in 20 films and was a teen idol in Hong Kong.

unusual to see him walking along the street throwing punches at the air and kicking leaves off trees.

In high school, Bruce was encouraged by a friend to enter the inter-school boxing championships. He had never put on gloves before, but amazingly knocked out the three-time champion.

In the same year he also won the Crown Colony Cha-Cha Championship. He was a great dancer and mastered the cha-cha by knowing how to do more than 100 steps.

Still, Bruce could not avoid the lure of fighting in the streets, alleys, and even in illegal rooftop contests. One of those contests got him into deep trouble with the police when he seriously injured a boy. A police detective warned his parents, "If Bruce gets into one more fight, I'm going to have to put him in jail."

But the streets of Hong Kong were a rough place to grow up. And Bruce ran with gangs of Chinese youths.

Chapter 3
A New Beginning

Lee's parents didn't want to risk their son going to jail. So they quickly decided to send him to the United States. He was 18 when he moved to Seattle, Washington in April, 1959. He lived with a friend of the family, Ruby Chow, a well-known restaurant owner, in a room above her restaurant. He attended Edison Technical School during the day to earn his high school diploma and waited tables at the restaurant at night. He still regularly practiced his kung fu, even while he worked, sometimes setting up a pad in the back of the kitchen and working on his "kata" (form). He also taught kung fu to many of his friends in backyards and city parks.

In 1961, Bruce was admitted to the University of Washington and taught kung fu to students there. One student was Taky Kimura, a 38-year-old Japanese-American businessman. A friend told him about this gifted martial artist named Bruce Lee. "I was so amazed and impressed by his ability that I immediately asked him if I could join his club," Taky said. Kimura became a lifelong friend.

His pupils often wore gym clothes while they practiced. There was no traditional ranking system such as brown belt or black belt. He believed that unless you could really do something, the only good thing about wearing a belt was to hold up your pants.

Bruce didn't believe any specific style should stand in the way of a martial artist fulfilling his or her potential. He told *Black Belt Magazine*

In 1961, Bruce was admitted to the University of Washington and he taught kung fu to students there.

that he considered classical forms too mechanical because they didn't prepare a student for actual combat.

"A guy could get clobbered while getting into his classical mess," he said once. Comments like this annoyed established martial arts masters who spent their entire lives focused on one particular style. Some of them viewed Bruce as being brash and cocky, others said that he was just very confident.

Bruce taught many classes in kung fu, but he was criticized by the Chinese community for teaching "outsiders."

Bob Wall, a karate instructor, friend, and later an actor in Bruce Lee's films once commented, "The one thing I hate about Bruce is that he can do anything." Taky Kimura added, "A lot of people took exception, but when they saw what he could do, they all wanted to join him."

Another person who joined Bruce's class was a thin, quiet, and blonde-haired woman named Linda Emery. One day after class, Bruce asked Linda if she would like to go out with him. Heart pounding, she accepted, and their first date was dinner at the famous Space Needle. They fell in love and were married on August 17, 1964. At first, her mother (Linda's father died when she was five) disapproved because Bruce was Chinese and her daughter was a Caucasian, or white person. Eventually she grew to love Bruce and accepted him as a member of her family.

Bruce met his wife Linda when she joined one of his classes.

Chapter 4 Conflict and Change

After they were married, Bruce and Linda moved to Oakland, California and planned on opening up a chain of kung fu schools. Bruce immediately ran into conflict with the elders in San Francisco's Chinese community who found out he was teaching kung fu to "outsiders." At the time, most Chinese martial arts teachers refused to teach anyone outside of their race. But Bruce Lee didn't care about color. He told potential students, "If your heart is right, I'm going to teach you."

These teachers told Bruce that he either had to stop or have a contest with

Bruce planned to set up a chain of kung fu schools.

their top fighter. Lee accepted the challenge and easily won when he put his opponent flat on his back on the mat in three minutes.

However, Bruce was disappointed by his performance. He felt that he should have won in a few seconds, not minutes. This fight became a significant event in his life and he took a hard look at the art of combat and his own physical condition. He realized that combat is an ever-changing process and you cannot expect to fight in a one-dimensional way.

Bruce and wife, Linda.

Inspired to become the best possible martial artist, Lee committed himself to an intense program of physical conditioning. It included running, jumping rope, calisthenics, punching bags, lifting weights (not for bulk, but for speed and power), improving his variety of kicks and lightning-fast reflexes, and developing new personal training equipment.

Bruce was also conscious of his health, so he was careful to eat nutritious foods and take many vitamins. He spent hours in libraries and bookstores reading, studying human anatomy, and exploring diverse fighting styles such as karate, tae kwon do, judo, jujitsu, wrestling, fencing, and Western boxing.

Film star and martial artist Chuck Norris stated, "No other human being trained the way Bruce trained — fanatically. He was a genius at creating new ideas. When he started working on some type of apparatus, he wouldn't stop until he became an expert at it."

Bruce practiced his kicks and various moves to perfection.

Chapter 5
Hollywood

A turning point in Bruce's life occurred when he was invited to perform at the first Ed Parker International Karate Championships in Long Beach. He astounded the crowd with his martial arts ability, physical prowess, and magnetic personality. As Ed Parker remembered, "He could make the air pop when he hit." Fortunately the demonstration was captured on film.

That film was shown to a television producer named William Dozier, who was famous for the *Batman* series. Dozier called Lee in for a screen test and cast him in a new television series based

Bruce's life changed when he was cast for a new television series.

on the successful *Green Hornet* radio serial of the 1930s. Bruce was delighted to get the part because his family had been struggling to pay its bills. Plus he was the proud father of a new son, Brandon Bruce Lee, born on February 1, 1965. Lee jokingly referred to him as "the only blonde-haired, gray-eyed Chinaman in the world."

Sadly, Bruce's father died a week after his grandson was born. Bruce flew to Hong Kong alone for his funeral.

The Lee family moved to Los Angeles in the spring of 1966 to film the *Green Hornet*. Bruce played the role of Kato, the Hornet's sidekick and driver. That gave television viewers their introduction to kung fu. Bruce sensationalized it with flying fists and feet. His movements

Van Williams (right) is presented by Adam West (left) the caped crusader of Batman. *In the center is Bruce Lee, who played Kato, the Green Hornet's faithful servant.*

were so quick that he was asked to slow down so the camera could catch the action without turning it into a blur.

Unfortunately, the series was canceled after one year. Bruce was depressed and struggled to find parts on TV shows including *Ironside*, *Blondie*, and *Here Comes the Brides*. He also appeared in the feature film *Marlowe*. He worked as technical advisor on several films, helping stars like Dean Martin and Sharon Tate.

Bruce Lee (right) as Kato in The Green Hornet.

On April 19, 1969, his daughter Shannon was born and it became an even more difficult time financially. Bruce reluctantly returned to teaching, opening a kwoon in Los Angeles's Chinatown. Lee also offered private instruction to such celebrities as actors Steve McQueen, Lee Marvin, James Coburn, and James Garner; filmmaker

Roman Polanski; writer/producer Sterling Silliphant; and basketball legend Kareem Abdul-Jabbar. Bruce's client list also included karate champions Joe Lewis, Chuck Norris, and Mike Stone.

During a weightlifting session in 1970, Lee suffered a severe back injury that left him bedridden for six months. The doctors said he would never kick again. It was a scary and frustrating time for Bruce, but he strongly believed in the power of positive thinking and had faith that his body would heal.

While he recuperated, Bruce wrote constantly, documenting his training methods and his philosophy of Jeet Kune Do (the way of the intercepting fist), a new martial arts fighting method he

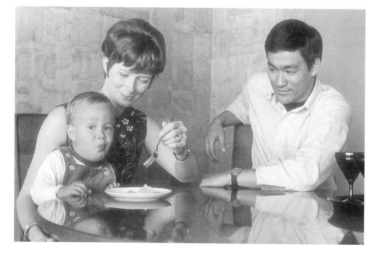

Bruce, Linda and baby Brandon.

created that incorporates numerous combat styles.

Bruce gradually regained his strength and proved the doctors wrong. He resumed his fitness program with even more vigor and directed his energies once again toward becoming an international film star.

But he had one last stumbling block to overcome. Hollywood producers believed that no Asian person could ever become a major movie star.

During his recovery from his back injury, Bruce worked on an idea about a Shaolin priest, a master of kung fu, who roams America's Old West. He had talks with Warner Brothers Studio and contributed many valuable ideas toward the development of the series. It resulted in the television show *Kung Fu.*

However, the starring role was given to a Caucasian actor, David Carradine, who had no martial arts experience. The studio never seriously considered using Bruce as the star. They claimed that he was "too Chinese."

Bruce had one last stumbling block to overcome. Hollywood producers believed that no Asian person could ever become a major movie star.

Lee was hurt by this rejection, but he continued to push forward. He found work on a new TV detective series called *Longstreet*. In the first episode, Li Tsung (Lee's character, an antique dealer) protects a blind detective from three thugs. The detective Li to teach him Jeet Kune Do. The role perfectly showcased Bruce's skills. Appropriately, the episode was called "The Way of the Intercepting Fist."

Bruce received excellent reviews for his acting from newspapers that reported on the film industry as well as the *Los Angeles* and *New York Times*. He also received more fan mail than the star, James Franciscus. The producers were delighted with Lee's performance and offered him a regular role in the series. But by the time the show aired Bruce was about to become the biggest box office draw in the Far East.

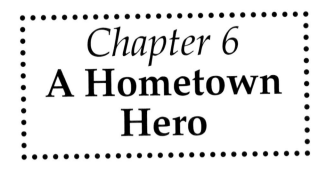

Chapter 6
A Hometown Hero

Prior to filming *Longstreet*, Bruce took a trip to Hong Kong with his five-year-old son, Brandon. It was his first trip back home in several years, and when he arrived he was stunned by the tremendous reception he received. Bruce didn't realize that *Green Hornet* was the most popular show in Southeast Asia. It was referred to as the "Kato Show." Fans swarmed their hometown hero and the media besieged him with interview requests. Bruce loved his newfound celebrity and in the interviews his charm, charisma, and wit came to the

When Bruce returned to Hong Kong for a trip, he found he was a hero.

surface. Soon movie producers in Hong Kong and Taiwan began to call him.

Bruce signed a contract with producer Raymond Chow of Golden Harvest Productions and flew to Bangkok, Thailand in 1971 to shoot his first starring role in *The Big Boss*. He also choreographed the fight scenes, telling the actors what to do and when to do it. *The Big Boss* (released in the U.S. as *Fists of Fury*) smashed box office records throughout Asia. Within three weeks it soared past the previous record-breaker, *The Sound of Music*, grossing over three and a half million dollars in Hong Kong.

In 1971, Bruce, Linda, Brandon, and Shannon moved to an apartment in Hong Kong while he filmed his second movie, *The Chinese Connection*. It, too, shattered box office records and Lee's celebrity skyrocketed. On opening night so many Bruce Lee movie fans rushed the theater in Singapore that it produced a massive traffic jam and the movie was canceled for a week until the problems were solved.

Soon movie producers in Hong Kong and Taiwan began to call him.

Lee's next movie, *Way of the Dragon*, also did spectacular business and was the first Hong Kong movie to ever go to Europe for location shooting. The film's highlight was the battle between Bruce Lee and Chuck Norris in the home of the gladiators — the Colosseum in Rome, Italy.

After departing from Italy, Lee began working on the concept of his next feature film, *Game of Death*. Meanwhile, in 1972, Fists *of Fury* and *The Chinese Connection* opened in the United States. Hollywood bigshots noticed, particularly when people in the theater hysterically clapped, screamed, and leaped to their feet when their hero battled anywhere up to 50 men.

Suddenly, Hollywood had a new attitude about the man it once claimed had no box office value because he was "too Chinese." Producer Fred Weintraub flew to Hong Kong to meet with Lee and the two men signed a co-production deal.

Suddenly, Hollywood had a new attitude about the man it once claimed had no box office value because he was "too Chinese."

Chapter 7
The Immortal Dragon

Bruce was not prepared for the pressures and demands that came with being famous.

Lee stopped working on the *Game of Death* and began production on his first Warner Brothers movie, *Blood and Steel*. Although he was exhausted, Bruce was too excited and thrilled to rest. He knew he was about to realize his dream. To mark his arrival, he changed the name of the film to *Enter the Dragon*.

Bruce Lee — movie star, writer, stunt choreographer, director, producer, philosopher, and extraordinary martial artist — was on the verge of accomplishing even more than he had ever dreamed. But he wasn't prepared for the daily pressures and demands that came with being famous.

Furthermore, his perfectionism and excessive work habits caused him to suffer weight loss, severe mood swings, sleeplessness, and constant headaches. Bruce was involved in every aspect of filming *Enter the Dragon* and it took up most of his energy.

Filming on *Enter the Dragon* was completed by April 1973 and Lee started back to work on *Game of Death*. On May 10, while editing the final print of *Enter the Dragon* in a Hong Kong studio, Lee became dizzy and collapsed. Rushed to the hospital, he appeared very close to death but regained consciousness the next day. In June, he flew to UCLA for a battery of tests. The doctors gave him a clean bill of health.

On July 20, 1973, Bruce Lee was discussing the *Game of Death* script with actress Betty Ting-pei in her apartment. He began complaining that he had a headache, so she gave him a type of aspirin to reduce the pain. He went into

On July 20, 1973, Bruce was discussing the script for *Game of Death* with actress Betty Ting-pei when he began complaining of a headache.

her bedroom to lie down and take a nap. But he never woke up.

Doctors who examined his body said that the immediate cause of death was a cerebral edema (swelling of the brain). However, no one could figure out the exact cause of the cerebral edema and Lee's death is still surrounded by controversy.

Doctors said his cause of death was swelling of the brain.

Five days later, 25,000 people attended Bruce Lee's funeral. Afterwards, his body was flown to Seattle where it rests today. He was buried in the Chinese outfit he had worn in *Enter the Dragon*.

Sadly, 20 years later, on March 31, 1993, his only son, Brandon, who was on the road to becoming a major film star himself, was accidentally killed on a movie set by a bullet fired from a gun that was supposed to have contained blanks. His grave lies next to his father's.

After its release, *Enter the Dragon* became Warner Brothers' highest grossing movie of 1973. It has earned well over $400 million and hundreds of thousands of people come to see Bruce Lee films annually with almost a religious reverence.

Bruce Lee's achievements are unparalleled. He advanced the martial arts by daring to question its very principles and foundations. A quote by St. Augustine, who lived in the Middle Ages, is featured in the last frame of the film biography *Dragon: The Bruce Lee Story*. It best sums up his short life:

The key to immortality is living a life worth remembering.

The key to immortality is living a life worth remem— bering.

Selected Film and Television Credits

- 1940 *Golden Gate Girl* (baby "stand-in," an American production)
- 1946 *The Beginning of a Boy* (professional screen debut at six)
- 1958 *The Orphan* (Lee's 20th and last film as a child star)
- 1966-1967 *The Green Hornet* (30 half-hour shows)
- 1967-1970 appears in television shows *Ironside, Blondie, Here Come the Brides; Marlowe* (feature film)
- 1971 *Longstreet* (4 TV episodes); *The Big Boss* (U.S. film release called *Fist of Fury*)
- 1972 *Fist of Fury* (U.S. release, The *Chinese Connection*); The *Way of the Dragon* (*Return of the Dragon* in U.S.)
- 1973 *Enter The Dragon*
- 1978 *Game of Death* (posthumously released — Bruce completed only 20 minutes of film. Bruce Lee look-alikes were used for the additional 80 minutes)

Chronology

- 1940, born November 27 in San Francisco to Lee Hoi Chuen, a well-known film and stage actor, and Grace Li.
- 1946, appears in the first of his 20 childhood films at the age of six.
- 1952, after elementary school, attends La Salle College (a Catholic boys school) at the age of 12 and turns to the streets for excitement.
- 1953, trains in martial arts under renowned kung fu master, Sifu Yip Man, after several violent clashes with street gangs.
- 1958, wins the Inter-school Boxing Championship of Hong Kong; also wins the Colony Cha-Cha Championship.
- 1959, after a serious fighting incident, Lee's parents send him to Seattle, Washington.
- 1961, receives his high school degree from Edison Technical Institute and enters the University of Washington.
- 1963, opens his first Jun Fan Kung Fu Institute.
- 1964, marries his former student, Linda Emery, and the couple moves to Oakland, California.
- 1965, Linda gives birth to Brandon Bruce Lee; a week later, Bruce's father dies.
- 1966, moves to Los Angeles to star as Kato on the *Green Hornet*.
- 1969, Linda gives birth to daughter, Shannon Lee; Bruce writes out his master plan.
- 1970, injures nerve in his back and is bedridden for six months; flies to Hong Kong and is stunned by tremendous reception from fans and media; is offered starring roles in Hong Kong films.
- 1971, flies to Bangkok to shoot *The Big Boss*; which shatters box office records in Asia; becomes a superstar.
- 1972, makes *Fists of Fury* and *The Way of the Dragon*.
- 1973, films *Enter The Dragon*; dies on July 20 and is heralded as "world's greatest martial artist."

Index